The Bible Overview

HOW TO UNDERSTAND THE BIBLE AS A WHOLE

Written by Matthew Brain, Matthew A. Malcolm,
Matthew R. Malcolm and Greg Clarke

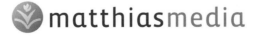

The Bible Overview
© M. Brain, M. A. Malcolm, M. R. Malcolm, Matthias Media, 2001.
Original artwork by Immki Quek and Ollie Lindsell.

Matthias Media
(St Matthias Press Ltd ACN 067 558 365)
PO Box 225
Kingsford NSW 2032
Australia
Telephone: (02) 9663 1478; international: +61-2-9663-1478
Facsimile: (02) 9663 3265; international: +61-2-9663-3265
Email: info@matthiasmedia.com.au
Internet: www.matthiasmedia.com.au

Matthias Media (USA)
Telephone: 724 964 8152; international: +1-724-964-8152
Facsimile: 724 964 8166; international: +1-724-964- 8166
Email: sales@matthiasmedia.com
Internet: www.matthiasmedia.com

ISBN 978 1 876326 34 0

Cover design and typesetting by Lankshear Design Pty Ltd.

Welcome to The Bible Overview

Have you ever tried putting together a jigsaw puzzle without a picture of what it is meant to look like when it is all assembled?

It is almost impossible to fit the pieces together properly unless you know what you are aiming for.

This short course is designed to give you an understanding of the Bible as a whole. Like the jigsaw, it is much harder to understand any one part of the Bible if you don't have some grasp of the whole book. Once you have this overview of the book, some of the smaller parts don't seem so confusing or difficult to understand.

This is a course for everyone, from children to grandparents, from students of the Bible to those who are reading it for the first time. It is designed to work like a guided tour. We provide a map, explain the route, and point out landmarks and signposts along the way. It is our hope that this will mean that you can come back to the Bible on your own, confident that you know the terrain.

May God reward you on your travels.

M. Brain, M. A. Malcolm, M. R. Malcolm, G. Clarke

CONTENTS

I nside the pages of this booklet, you will find the 15 stages of the unfolding story of the Bible as they will be explained during *The Bible Overview* presentations. To explain each stage, we have included:

- a verse or two from the Bible which introduces or summarizes the stage
- a picture and summary word to make it easy to remember the details of each stage
- a short explanation of what the stage is about, so that you can remind yourself of it after the course is finished
- a few extra Bible verses for use in the Old Testament and New Testament presentations.

After these 15 stages, there is a chart showing how these stages are connected with each other. During the course of *The Bible Overview* presentations, your course leader will construct this diagram on a screen, or a display board or wall, using pictures which match the ones in your book. The last few pages of the booklet provide a one-paragraph summary of the story of the Bible and a quick-reference chart for using the COMA method of understanding a Bible passage.

CREATION

GENESIS 1:31-2:1

[31] God saw all that he had made, and it was very good. And there was evening, and there was morning—the sixth day. [2:1] Thus the heavens and the earth were completed in all their vast array.

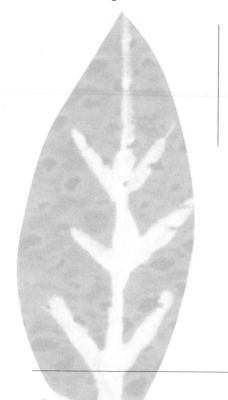

God made the world and everything in it, and he made humans in his own image. The first humans were Adam and Eve. As Creator of the world, God is the ruler (or king) of it. However, God blessed Adam and Eve and appointed them to be rulers over his creation.

Who God is

GENESIS 1:1

[1] In the beginning God created the heavens and the earth.

JOHN 1:1-4

[1] In the beginning was the Word, and the Word was with God, and the Word was God. [2] He was with God in the beginning. [3] Through him all things were made; without him nothing was made that has been made. [4] In him was life, and that life was the light of men.

What God does

GENESIS 1:27-31

[27] So God created man in his own image, in the image of God he created him; male and female he created them. [28] God blessed them and said to them, "Be fruitful and increase in number; fill the earth and subdue it. Rule over the fish of the sea and the birds of the air and over every living creature that moves on the ground." [29] Then God said, "I give you every seed-bearing plant on the face of the whole earth and every tree that has fruit with seed in it. They will be yours for food. [30] And to all the beasts of the earth and all the birds of the air and all the creatures that move on the ground—everything that has the breath of life in it—I give every green plant for food." And it was so.

[31] God saw all that he had made, and it was very good. And there was evening, and there was morning—the sixth day.

How God works

PSALM 33:9

[9] For he spoke, and it came to be; he commanded, and it stood firm.

HEBREWS 11:3

[3] By faith we understand that the universe was formed at God's command, so that what is seen was not made out of what was visible.

THE FALL

GENESIS 11:4

⁴ Then they said, "Come, let us build ourselves a city, with a tower that reaches to the heavens, so that we may make a name for ourselves and not be scattered over the face of the whole earth".

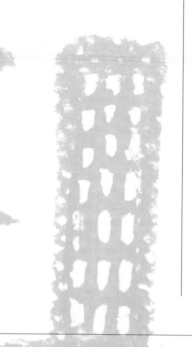

Adam and Eve chose to reject God their ruler (or king). The effects of rejecting God were devastating. As a result, humans no longer relate rightly to God, to each other, or to the creation in which we've been placed.

The people tried to build a tower so huge that they could make a "name" for themselves apart from God. People followed in Adam and Eve's footsteps, crying out to God, "We know better—we'll do things *our* way!" God's response to humanity's actions at Babel was to confuse their language, so that they could not complete the tower, and to scatter them over the whole earth.

Who God is

GENESIS 6:5-6

5 The LORD saw how great man's wickedness on the earth had become, and that every inclination of the thoughts of his heart was only evil all the time. 6 The LORD was grieved that he had made man on the earth, and his heart was filled with pain.

ROMANS 1:18-20

18 The wrath of God is being revealed from heaven against all the godlessness and wickedness of men who suppress the truth by their wickedness, 19 since what may be known about God is plain to them, because God has made it plain to them. 20 For since the creation of the world God's invisible qualities—his eternal power and divine nature—have been clearly seen, being understood from what has been made, so that men are without excuse.

What God does

GENESIS 3:14-19

14 So the LORD God said to the serpent, "Because you have done this, "Cursed are you above all the livestock and all the wild animals! You will crawl on your belly and you will eat dust all the days of your life. 15 And I will put enmity between you and the woman, and between your offspring and hers; he will crush your head, and you will strike his heel."

16 To the woman he said, "I will greatly increase your pains in childbearing; with pain you will give birth to children. Your desire will be for your husband, and he will rule over you."

17 To Adam he said, "Because you listened to your wife and ate from the tree about which I commanded you, 'You must not eat of it', "cursed is the ground because of you; through painful toil you will eat of it all the days of your life. 18 It will produce thorns and thistles for you, and you will eat the plants of the field. 19 By the sweat of your brow you will eat your food until you return to the ground, since from it you were taken; for dust you are and to dust you will return."

ROMANS 5:12

12 Therefore, just as sin entered the world through one man, and death through sin, and in this way death came to all men, because all sinned ...

How God works

GENESIS 11:8-9

8 So the LORD scattered them from there over all the earth, and they stopped building the city. 9 That is why it was called Babel—because there the LORD confused the language of the whole world. From there the LORD scattered them over the face of the whole earth.

THE PLEDGE

GENESIS 12:1-3

¹The Lord had said to Abram, "Leave your country, your people and your father's household and go to the land I will show you. ²I will make you into a great nation and I will bless you; I will make your name great, and you will be a blessing. ³I will bless those who bless you, and whoever curses you I will curse; and all peoples on earth will be blessed through you."

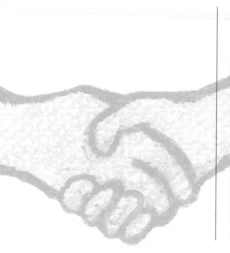

God chose one man, Abraham, and made a special pledge to him (also called a 'covenant' or 'promise'). Whereas at Babel, the people had sought to make a name for themselves, God promised to make a "name" for Abraham, and pledged to him a special relationship. God would make a great nation from Abraham's descendants, and give them a land of their own. He did this so that in the end, the whole world would be blessed, and humanity's rejection of God would not go on forever.

Who God is

GENESIS 12:1-3 *(see opposite page)*

GALATIANS 3:6-9

[6] Consider Abraham: "He believed God, and it was credited to him as righteousness". [7] Understand, then, that those who believe are children of Abraham. [8] The Scripture foresaw that God would justify the Gentiles by faith, and announced the gospel in advance to Abraham: "All nations will be blessed through you". [9] So those who have faith are blessed along with Abraham, the man of faith.

What God does

GENESIS 17:7

[7] I will establish my covenant as an everlasting covenant between me and you and your descendants after you for the generations to come, to be your God and the God of your descendants after you.

HEBREWS 6:13-20

[13] When God made his promise to Abraham, since there was no one greater for him to swear by, he swore by himself, [14] saying, "I will surely bless you and give you many descendants". [15] And so after waiting patiently, Abraham received what was promised.

[16] Men swear by someone greater than themselves, and the oath confirms what is said and puts an end to all argument. [17] Because God wanted to make the unchanging nature of his purpose very clear to the heirs of what was promised, he confirmed it with an oath. [18] God did this so that, by two unchangeable things in which it is impossible for God to lie, we who have fled to take hold of the hope offered to us may be greatly encouraged. [19] We have this hope as an anchor for the soul, firm and secure. It enters the inner sanctuary behind the curtain, [20] where Jesus, who went before us, has entered on our behalf. He has become a high priest forever, in the order of Melchizedek.

How God works

GENESIS 15:5-6

[5] He took him outside and said, "Look up at the heavens and count the stars— if indeed you can count them". Then he said to him, "So shall your offspring be".

[6] Abram believed the LORD, and he credited it to him as righteousness.

GALATIANS 3:6-7

[6] Consider Abraham: "He believed God, and it was credited to him as righteousness". [7] Understand, then, that those who believe are children of Abraham.

EXODUS FROM SLAVERY

EXODUS 2:23-24

²³ During that long period, the king of Egypt died. The Israelites groaned in their slavery and cried out, and their cry for help because of their slavery went up to God. ²⁴ God heard their groaning and he remembered his covenant with Abraham, with Isaac and with Jacob.

EXODUS 14:29-30

²⁹ But the Israelites went through the sea on dry ground, with a wall of water on their right and on their left.
³⁰ That day the LORD saved Israel from the hands of the Egyptians, and Israel saw the Egyptians lying dead on the shore.

Abraham's descendants became known as "Israel". They went to Egypt, and there they were made slaves for about 400 years. But God had not forgotten his pledge to Abraham. God saved his people Israel from slavery in Egypt, by bringing them through the sea.

Who God is

EXODUS 6:2-8

² God also said to Moses, "I am the LORD. ³ I appeared to Abraham, to Isaac and to Jacob as God Almighty, but by my name the LORD I did not make myself known to them. ⁴ I also established my covenant with them to give them the land of Canaan, where they lived as aliens. ⁵ Moreover, I have heard the groaning of the Israelites, whom the Egyptians are enslaving, and I have remembered my covenant.

⁶ "Therefore, say to the Israelites: 'I am the LORD, and I will bring you out from under the yoke of the Egyptians. I will free you from being slaves to them, and I will redeem you with an outstretched arm and with mighty acts of judgment. ⁷ I will take you as my own people, and I will be your God. Then you will know that I am the LORD your God, who brought you out from under the yoke of the Egyptians. ⁸ And I will bring you to the land I swore with uplifted hand to give to Abraham, to Isaac and to Jacob. I will give it to you as a possession. I am the LORD.'"

What God does

EXODUS 20:1-2

¹ And God spoke all these words: ² "I am the LORD your God, who brought you out of Egypt, out of the land of slavery."

How God works

EXODUS 15:7-10

⁷ "In the greatness of your majesty you threw down those who opposed you. You unleashed your burning anger; it consumed them like stubble. ⁸ By the blast of your nostrils the waters piled up. The surging waters stood firm like a wall; the deep waters congealed in the heart of the sea. ⁹ The enemy boasted, 'I will pursue, I will overtake them. I will divide the spoils; I will gorge myself on them. I will draw my sword and my hand will destroy them.' ¹⁰ But you blew with your breath, and the sea covered them. They sank like lead in the mighty waters."

1 PETER 2:9-10

⁹ But you are a chosen people, a royal priesthood, a holy nation, a people belonging to God, that you may declare the praises of him who called you out of darkness into his wonderful light. ¹⁰ Once you were not a people, but now you are the people of God; once you had not received mercy, but now you have received mercy.

THE PROMISED LAND

DEUTERONOMY 26:8-9

[8] "So the LORD brought us out of Egypt with a mighty hand and an outstretched arm, with great terror and with miraculous signs and wonders. [9] He brought us to this place and gave us this land, a land flowing with milk and honey."

God brought Israel through the sea in order to bring them to the land he had promised to Abraham and his descendants. They were to live as God's special people in this land he had given them. The promises to Abraham were beginning to be fulfilled: there was a nation of descendants who were to receive the Promised Land.

Who God is

EXODUS 34:10-14

[10] Then the LORD said: "I am making a covenant with you. Before all your people I will do wonders never before done in any nation in all the world. The people you live among will see how awesome is the work that I, the LORD, will do for you. [11] Obey what I command you today. I will drive out before you the Amorites, Canaanites, Hittites, Perizzites, Hivites and Jebusites. [12] Be careful not to make a treaty with those who live in the land where you are going, or they will be a snare among you. [13] Break down their altars, smash their sacred stones and cut down their Asherah poles. [14] Do not worship any other god, for the LORD, whose name is Jealous, is a jealous God."

What God does

EXODUS 6:8

[8] "And I will bring you to the land I swore with uplifted hand to give to Abraham, to Isaac and to Jacob. I will give it to you as a possession. I am the LORD.'"

How God works

EXODUS 15:17-18

[17] "You will bring them in and plant them on the mountain of your inheritance—the place, O LORD, you made for your dwelling, the sanctuary, O Lord, your hands established. [18] The LORD will reign for ever and ever."

THE LAW

DEUTERONOMY 6:1-2

[1] "These are the commands, decrees and laws the LORD your God directed me to teach you to observe in the land that you are crossing the Jordan to possess, [2] so that you, your children and their children after them may fear the LORD your God as long as you live by keeping all his decrees and commands that I give you, and so that you may enjoy long life."

On their way to the Promised Land, Israel was given instructions on how to live in their new land. These instructions told Israel about what it meant to be in a special relationship with their God. The law told them how to live as God's saved people—how to live as the people through whom the whole world would ultimately be blessed. The most famous part of the Old Testament law is the Ten Commandments.

Who God is

EXODUS 34:4-7

⁴So Moses chiselled out two stone tablets like the first ones and went up Mount Sinai early in the morning, as the LORD had commanded him; and he carried the two stone tablets in his hands. ⁵ Then the LORD came down in the cloud and stood there with him and proclaimed his name, the LORD. ⁶ And he passed in front of Moses, proclaiming, "The LORD, the LORD, the compassionate and gracious God, slow to anger, abounding in love and faithfulness, ⁷ maintaining love to thousands, and forgiving wickedness, rebellion and sin. Yet he does not leave the guilty unpunished; he punishes the children and their children for the sin of the fathers to the third and fourth generation."

What God does

DEUTERONOMY 6:20-25

²⁰ "In the future, when your son asks you, 'What is the meaning of the stipulations, decrees and laws the LORD our God has commanded you?' ²¹ tell him: 'We were slaves of Pharaoh in Egypt, but the LORD brought us out of Egypt with a mighty hand. ²² Before our eyes the LORD sent miraculous signs and wonders—great and terrible—upon Egypt and Pharaoh and his whole household. ²³ But he brought us out from there to bring us in and give us the land that he promised on oath to our forefathers. ²⁴ The LORD commanded us to obey all these decrees and to fear the LORD our God, so that we might always prosper and be kept alive, as is the case today. ²⁵ And if we are careful to obey all this law before the LORD our God, as he has commanded us, that will be our righteousness.' "

How God works

EXODUS 19:3-6

³ Then Moses went up to God, and the LORD called to him from the mountain and said, "This is what you are to say to the house of Jacob and what you are to tell the people of Israel: ⁴ 'You yourselves have seen what I did to Egypt, and how I carried you on eagles' wings and brought you to myself. ⁵ Now if you obey me fully and keep my covenant, then out of all nations you will be my treasured possession. Although the whole earth is mine, ⁶ you will be for me a kingdom of priests and a holy nation.' These are the words you are to speak to the Israelites."

KINGS

1 SAMUEL 12:13-14

[13]"Now here is the king you have chosen, the one you asked for; see, the LORD has set a king over you. [14] If you fear the LORD and serve and obey him and do not rebel against his commands, and if both you and the king who reigns over you follow the LORD your God—good!"

While they were in the Promised Land, God gave Israel kings. The king's role was to be God's 'representative' on earth by ruling Israel and saving them in battle. The most famous king of Israel was David. The king also represented Israel before God.

Who God is

2 SAMUEL 7:12-16

¹²"When your days are over and you rest with your fathers, I will raise up your offspring to succeed you, who will come from your own body, and I will establish his kingdom. ¹³ He is the one who will build a house for my Name, and I will establish the throne of his kingdom forever. ¹⁴ I will be his father, and he will be my son. When he does wrong, I will punish him with the rod of men, with floggings inflicted by men. ¹⁵ But my love will never be taken away from him, as I took it away from Saul, whom I removed from before you. ¹⁶ Your house and your kingdom will endure forever before me; your throne will be established forever."

What God does

1 SAMUEL 12:13-14 *(see opposite page)*

How God works

1 KINGS 9:4-7

⁴ "As for you, if you walk before me in integrity of heart and uprightness, as David your father did, and do all I command and observe my decrees and laws, ⁵ I will establish your royal throne over Israel forever, as I promised David your father when I said, 'You shall never fail to have a man on the throne of Israel'.

⁶ "But if you or your sons turn away from me and do not observe the commands and decrees I have given you and go off to serve other gods and worship them, ⁷ then I will cut off Israel from the land I have given them and will reject this temple I have consecrated for my Name. Israel will then become a byword and an object of ridicule among all peoples."

PSALM 2:7-12

⁷ I will proclaim the decree of the LORD:
He said to me, "You are my Son; today I have become your Father.

⁸ Ask of me, and I will make the nations your inheritance, the ends of the earth your possession.

⁹ You will rule them with an iron sceptre; you will dash them to pieces like pottery."

¹⁰ Therefore, you kings, be wise; be warned, you rulers of the earth.

¹¹ Serve the LORD with fear and rejoice with trembling.

¹² Kiss the Son, lest he be angry and you be destroyed in your way, for his wrath can flare up in a moment. Blessed are all who take refuge in him.

EXILE

PSALM 137

¹ By the rivers of Babylon we sat and wept when we remembered Zion.

² There on the poplars we hung our harps,

³ for there our captors asked us for songs, our tormentors demanded songs of joy; they said, "Sing us one of the songs of Zion!"

⁴ How can we sing the songs of the LORD while in a foreign land?

⁵ If I forget you, O Jerusalem, may my right hand forget [its skill].

⁶ May my tongue cling to the roof of my mouth if I do not remember you, if I do not consider Jerusalem my highest joy.

⁷ Remember, O LORD, what the Edomites did on the day Jerusalem fell. "Tear it down", they cried, "tear it down to its foundations!"

⁸ O Daughter of Babylon, doomed to destruction, happy is he who repays you for what you have done to us—⁹ he who seizes your infants and dashes them against the rocks.

Throughout their history, God's people disobeyed the law and neglected their special relationship with God. Even the kings forgot about God. The very people through whom God planned to bring blessing to the world were thinking, "We know better, God—we'll do things *our* way". So God took them out of their Promised Land. He sent them away to the surrounding nations. While they were in exile, the people were in anguish, because it seemed that God's promises to Abraham were being undone. Many descendants were wiped out, and those who were left were banished from the Promised Land.

Who God is

2 KINGS 17:18-20

[18] So the LORD was very angry with Israel and removed them from his presence. Only the tribe of Judah was left, [19] and even Judah did not keep the commands of the LORD their God. They followed the practices Israel had introduced. [20] Therefore the LORD rejected all the people of Israel; he afflicted them and gave them into the hands of plunderers, until he thrust them from his presence.

LAMENTATIONS 4:22

[22] O Daughter of Zion, your punishment will end; he will not prolong your exile. But, O Daughter of Edom, he will punish your sin and expose your wickedness.

What God does

2 KINGS 17:35-41

[35] When the LORD made a covenant with the Israelites, he commanded them: "Do not worship any other gods or bow down to them, serve them or sacrifice to them. [36] But the LORD, who brought you up out of Egypt with mighty power and outstretched arm, is the one you must worship. To him you shall bow down and to him offer sacrifices. [37] You must always be careful to keep the decrees and ordinances, the laws and commands he wrote for you. Do not worship other gods. [38] Do not forget the covenant I have made with you, and do not worship other gods. [39] Rather, worship the LORD your God; it is he who will deliver you from the hand of all your enemies."

[40] They would not listen, however, but persisted in their former practices. [41] Even while these people were worshiping the LORD, they were serving their idols. To this day their children and grandchildren continue to do as their fathers did.

ROMANS 11:1-6

[1] I ask then: Did God reject his people? By no means! I am an Israelite myself, a descendant of Abraham, from the tribe of Benjamin. [2] God did not reject his people, whom he foreknew. Don't you know what the Scripture says in the passage about Elijah—how he appealed to God against Israel: [3] "Lord, they have killed your prophets and torn down your altars; I am the only one left, and they are trying to kill me"? [4] And what was God's answer to him? "I have reserved for myself seven thousand who have not bowed the knee to Baal." [5] So too, at the present time there is a remnant chosen by grace. [6] And if by grace, then it is no longer by works; if it were, grace would no longer be grace.

How God works

JEREMIAH 29:10-14

[10] This is what the LORD says: "When seventy years are completed for Babylon, I will come to you and fulfil my gracious promise to bring you back to this place. [11] For I know the plans I have for you", declares the LORD, "plans to prosper you and not to harm you, plans to give you hope and a future. [12] Then you will call upon me and come and pray to me, and I will listen to you. [13] You will seek me and find me when you seek me with all your heart. [14] I will be found by you", declares the LORD, "and will bring you back from captivity. I will gather you from all the nations and places where I have banished you", declares the LORD, "and will bring you back to the place from which I carried you into exile."

PROPHETS

JEREMIAH 31:31-33

[31] "The time is coming", declares the LORD, "when I will make a new covenant with the house of Israel and with the house of Judah. [32] It will not be like the covenant I made with their forefathers when I took them by the hand to lead them out of Egypt, because they broke my covenant, though I was a husband to them", declares the LORD. [33] "This is the covenant I will make with the house of Israel after that time", declares the LORD. "I will put my law in their minds and write it on their hearts. I will be their God, and they will be my people."

God spoke through prophets to call Israel back to their special relationship with God. The prophets reminded Israel that God had made a pledge with them. They explained that God's people had treated their God badly, and warned the people of God's anger and judgement. But the prophets also comforted the people, telling them that God would not forget his pledge to Abraham and his descendants. The prophets pointed forward to the ultimate fulfilment of this pledge.

Who God is

JEREMIAH 31:37

[37] This is what the LORD says: "Only if the heavens above can be measured and the foundations of the earth below be searched out will I reject all the descendants of Israel because of all they have done", declares the LORD.

What God does

HEBREWS 1:1

[1] In the past God spoke to our forefathers through the prophets at many times and in various ways ...

How God works

ISAIAH 48:1-11

[1] "Listen to this, O house of Jacob, you who are called by the name of Israel and come from the line of Judah, you who take oaths in the name of the LORD and invoke the God of Israel— but not in truth or righteousness— [2] you who call yourselves citizens of the holy city and rely on the God of Israel —the LORD Almighty is his name: [3] I foretold the former things long ago, my mouth announced them and I made them known; then suddenly I acted, and they came to pass. [4] For I knew how stubborn you were; the sinews of your neck were iron, your forehead was bronze. [5] Therefore I told you these things long ago; before they happened I announced them to you so that you could not say, 'My idols did them; my wooden image and metal god ordained them'.

[6] You have heard these things; look at them all. Will you not admit them? From now on I will tell you of new things, of hidden things unknown to you. [7] They are created now, and not long ago; you have not heard of them before today. So you cannot say, 'Yes, I knew of them'. [8] You have neither heard nor understood; from of old your ear has not been open. Well do I know how treacherous you are; you were called a rebel from birth.

[9] For my own name's sake I delay my wrath; for the sake of my praise I hold it back from you, so as not to cut you off. [10] See, I have refined you, though not as silver; I have tested you in the furnace of affliction. [11] For my own sake, for my own sake, I do this. How can I let myself be defamed? I will not yield my glory to another."

Why read the Old Testament?

Sometimes Christians wonder whether studying the Old Testament is a waste of time. It is not! It is worthwhile, in fact essential, for Christians to read and study the Old Testament for many reasons:

- In the Old Testament, as we have seen, we learn of the character, purposes and work of our God.
- It is the context God gave us for understanding Jesus and the New Testament. Jesus told his followers that the Old Testament was all about him (see Luke 24:25-27).
- New Testament writers used the Old Testament as the foundation of their instruction about Jesus, God, and his people.
- The Old Testament was written for our benefit. "For everything that was written in the past was written to teach us, so that through endurance and the encouragement of the Scriptures, we might have hope" (Rom 15:4; see also 2 Tim 3:16; 1 Pet 1:10-12).

NOTES

LIFE OF JESUS

LUKE 2:11

[11] "Today in the town of David a Saviour has been born to you; he is Christ the Lord."

MARK 1:14-15

[14] After John was put in prison, Jesus went into Galilee, proclaiming the good news of God. [15] "The time has come", he said. "The kingdom of God is near. Repent and believe the good news!"

God kept his pledge by sending his son Jesus into the world. Jesus was a Jew, an Israelite who was a descendant of King David. He lived the life of special relationship with God that all of Israel was supposed to live. He fulfilled the words of the prophets. Unlike Israel (and unlike Adam and Eve), Jesus never disobeyed God. He told people that it was time for God's people to be reconciled to him.

23 Jesus went throughout Galilee, teaching in their synagogues, preaching the good news of the kingdom, and healing every disease and sickness among the people.

Power

MARK 2:1-12

1 A few days later, when Jesus again entered Capernaum, the people heard that he had come home. 2 So many gathered that there was no room left, not even outside the door, and he preached the word to them. 3 Some men came, bringing to him a paralytic, carried by four of them. 4 Since they could not get him to Jesus because of the crowd, they made an opening in the roof above Jesus and, after digging through it, lowered the mat the paralysed man was lying on. 5 When Jesus saw their faith, he said to the paralytic, "Son, your sins are forgiven".

6 Now some teachers of the law were sitting there, thinking to themselves, 7 "Why does this fellow talk like that? He's blaspheming! Who can forgive sins but God alone?" 8 Immediately Jesus knew in his spirit that this was what they were thinking in their hearts, and he said to them, "Why are you thinking these things? 9 Which is easier: to say to the paralytic, 'Your sins are forgiven', or to say, 'Get up, take your mat and walk'? 10 But that you may know that the Son of Man has authority on earth to forgive sins ..." He said to the paralytic, 11 "I tell you, get up, take your mat and go home". 12 He got up, took his mat and walked out in full view of them all. This amazed everyone and they praised God, saying, "We have never seen anything like this!"

Preaching

LUKE 4:16-21

16 He went to Nazareth, where he had been brought up, and on the Sabbath day he went into the synagogue, as was his custom. And he stood up to read. 17 The scroll of the prophet Isaiah was handed to him. Unrolling it, he found the place where it is written: 18 "The Spirit of the Lord is on me, because he has anointed me to preach good news to the poor. He has sent me to proclaim freedom for the prisoners and recovery of sight for the blind, to release the oppressed, 19 to proclaim the year of the Lord's favour." 20 Then he rolled up the scroll, gave it back to the attendant and sat down. The eyes of everyone in the synagogue were fastened on him, 21 and he began by saying to them, "Today this scripture is fulfilled in your hearing".

MATTHEW 5:17

17 "Do not think that I have come to abolish the Law or the Prophets; I have not come to abolish them but to fulfill them."

Parables

MARK 4:11

11 He told them, "The secret of the kingdom of God has been given to you. But to those on the outside everything is said in parables."

DEATH OF JESUS

ROMANS 5:6-8

⁶ You see, at just the right time, when we were still powerless, Christ died for the ungodly. ⁷ Very rarely will anyone die for a righteous man, though for a good man someone might possibly dare to die. ⁸ But God demonstrates his own love for us in this: While we were still sinners, Christ died for us.

Jesus willingly died to take on himself the punishment due to humanity for their rejection of God. The Old Testament was pointing forward to this event. In the cross of Jesus, God the King was God the Saviour too. It was God's plan to demonstrate his love for his people by this act of self-sacrifice. It is an astonishing way to establish a kingdom.

[16] "For God so loved the world that he gave his one and only Son, that whoever believes in him shall not perish but have eternal life. [17] For God did not send his Son into the world to condemn the world, but to save the world through him."

RESURRECTION OF JESUS

1 CORINTHIANS 15:3-4

³ For what I received I passed on to you as of first importance: that Christ died for our sins according to the Scriptures, ⁴ that he was buried, that he was raised on the third day according to the Scriptures ...

God raised Jesus from death, showing that the penalty for disobedience had been paid and that the world could now be reconciled to God. After appearing to his followers, Jesus ascended to the right hand of God the Father, where he began his reign as the saving ruler of God's kingdom. His resurrection began the age of resurrection, in which God's people will inherit eternal life with Christ.

Jesus the Judge

ACTS 17:31

³¹ "For he has set a day when he will judge the world with justice by the man he has appointed. He has given proof of this to all men by raising him from the dead."

Jesus the Lord

ROMANS 1:3-4

³ ... regarding his Son, who as to his human nature was a descendant of David, ⁴ and who through the Spirit of holiness was declared with power to be the Son of God by his resurrection from the dead: Jesus Christ our Lord.

Jesus is glorified

PHILIPPIANS 2:9-11

⁹ Therefore God exalted him to the highest place and gave him the name that is above every name, ¹⁰ that at the name of Jesus every knee should bow, in heaven and on earth and under the earth, ¹¹ and every tongue confess that Jesus Christ is Lord, to the glory of God the Father.

1 PETER 1:21

²¹ Through him you believe in God, who raised him from the dead and glorified him, and so your faith and hope are in God.

PENTECOST

1 CORINTHIANS 2:12

¹² We have not received the spirit of the world but the Spirit who is from God, that we may understand what God has freely given us.

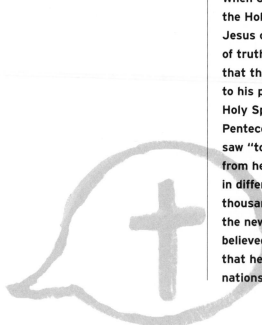

When Jesus returned to God, he sent the Holy Spirit to live in his followers. Jesus calls the Holy Spirit "the spirit of truth" (John 14:17) and tells us that the Spirit makes Christ known to his people and to the world. The Holy Spirit was given on the day of Pentecost, when a group of believers saw "tongues of fire" descend on them from heaven. They began to speak in different languages, and three thousand people in Jerusalem heard the news of the risen Christ and believed. God's pledge to Abraham, that he would provide a blessing to all nations, was being fulfilled.

Power to witness

ACTS 1:8

[8] "But you will receive power when the Holy Spirit comes on you; and you will be my witnesses in Jerusalem, and in all Judea and Samaria, and to the ends of the earth."

Spiritual fruit

GALATIANS 5:22-25

[22] But the fruit of the Spirit is love, joy, peace, patience, kindness, goodness, faithfulness, [23] gentleness and self-control. Against such things there is no law. [24] Those who belong to Christ Jesus have crucified the sinful nature with its passions and desires. [25] Since we live by the Spirit, let us keep in step with the Spirit.

Provision for the church

EPHESIANS 4:1-6

[1] As a prisoner for the Lord, then, I urge you to live a life worthy of the calling you have received. [2] Be completely humble and gentle; be patient, bearing with one another in love. [3] Make every effort to keep the unity of the Spirit through the bond of peace. [4] There is one body and one Spirit—just as you were called to one hope when you were called— [5] one Lord, one faith, one baptism; [6] one God and Father of all, who is over all and through all and in all.

RETURN OF JESUS

2 THESSALONIANS 1:8-10

⁸ He will punish those who do not know God and do not obey the gospel of our Lord Jesus. ⁹ They will be punished with everlasting destruction and shut out from the presence of the Lord and from the majesty of his power ¹⁰ on the day he comes to be glorified in his holy people and to be marveled at among all those who have believed. This includes you, because you believed our testimony to you.

Jesus will return as the powerful and glorious king. At that time, he will express the *fullness* of God's Kingdom by judging the whole world, and punishing 'Babel-ish' pride and rejection of God. But those who trust in Jesus will be saved from God's judgement and be with God forever. Until Jesus returns, his people are to live here in a manner worthy of the kingdom of God.

JOHN 14:3

³ And if I go and prepare a place for you, I will come back and take you to be with me that you also may be where I am.

NEW CREATION

REVELATION 21:3-4

³ And I heard a loud voice from the throne saying, "Now the dwelling of God is with men, and he will live with them. They will be his people, and God himself will be with them and be their God. ⁴ He will wipe every tear from their eyes. There will be no more death or mourning or crying or pain, for the old order of things has passed away."

After Jesus' return, God will make a new heavens and a new earth which will last forever. This can be thought of as the ultimate 'Promised Land'. Death and pain will be destroyed. God will dwell with his people in perfect fellowship in the kingdom he has made. God's plan for the world began with Creation and ends with the New Creation. Once again, God will rule as king, with his people ruling the New Creation under him.

REVELATION 21:1

[1] Then I saw a new heaven and a new earth, for the first heaven and the first earth had passed away, and there was no longer any sea.

REVELATION 21:22-23

[22] I did not see a temple in the city, because the Lord God Almighty and the Lamb are its temple. [23] The city does not need the sun or the moon to shine on it, for the glory of God gives it light, and the Lamb is its lamp.

1 CORINTHIANS 15:24-26

[24] Then the end will come, when he hands over the kingdom to God the Father after he has destroyed all dominion, authority and power. [25] For he must reign until he has put all his enemies under his feet. [26] The last enemy to be destroyed is death.

Living in the last days

L ife in the last days is marked by tension. It is sometimes referred to as the time of "now and not yet". We have the benefits of Christ's victory over sin and death *now*; but he has *not yet* returned in glory to judge the world.

You can explore this idea in the following Bible passages:

Now ...

- Romans 5:1 tells us that Christians are already justified and have peace with God.
- Ephesians 1:7 tells us that those who are in Christ already have redemption and forgiveness of sins.
- Romans 6:2 tells us that Christians have already died to sin.
- Philippians 3:20 tells us that we are already citizens of heaven.
- 2 Corinthians 5:17 tells us that those who are "in Christ" are already a "new creation", even though we still live in a fallen world.
- Colossians 3:1-4 tells us that our true life is now "hidden with Christ".
- 1 Thessalonians 5:1-11 tells us that Christians are to live now as people who belong to *that* day (the day of the Lord).

Not yet ...

- Romans 8:18-25 reminds us that we still live in a fallen world which groans for redemption, and that we also wait for the redemption of our bodies.
- 1 Corinthians 15:24-26 shows that while Christ is now reigning, we await the time when all his enemies will be destroyed.
- 1 Peter 2:21 shows that Christians will often experience unjust suffering.
- Revelation 20:4 reminds us that many Christians are killed because of their testimony about Jesus.

So the last days is a time of tension because there are things about the New Creation (the fullness of God's kingdom) that are true of us now, but there are many other things about the New Creation that we do not yet experience.

We already belong to God's kingdom and are saved, but we don't yet experience those things in their fullness. Although we are redeemed, forgiven and justified, we still sometimes get sick, we still experience pain and we still die. So we experience tension as we live a New Creation life in a Fallen, Babel-ish world.

GOD'S KINGDOM   God rules

FOUNDATION

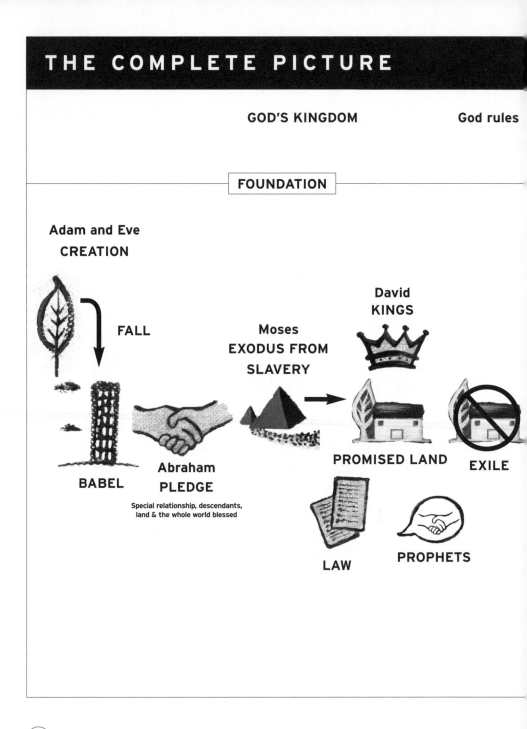

Adam and Eve
CREATION

FALL

Moses
EXODUS FROM
SLAVERY

David
KINGS

BABEL

Abraham
PLEDGE

Special relationship, descendants,
land & the whole world blessed

PROMISED LAND   EXILE

LAW   PROPHETS

God saves   **THROUGH JESUS**

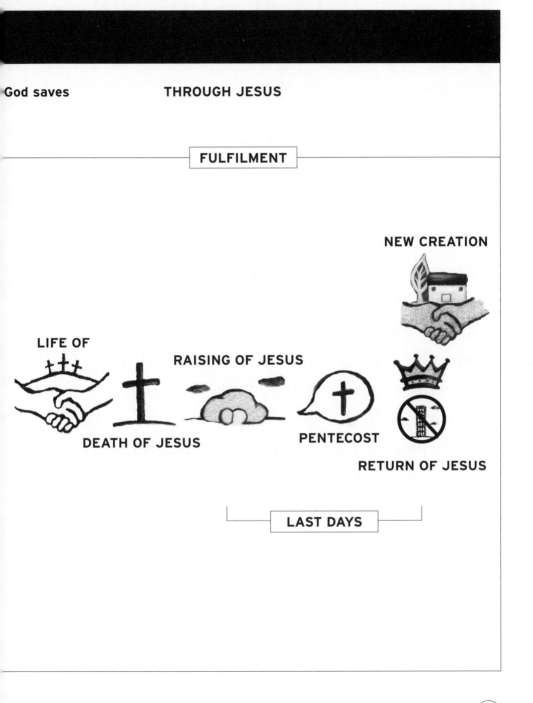

FULFILMENT

NEW CREATION

LIFE OF

RAISING OF JESUS

DEATH OF JESUS

PENTECOST

RETURN OF JESUS

LAST DAYS

The Bible Overview

We have produced an outline of the Bible that can be summarized like this:

> The Bible tells us that God appointed Jesus Christ as the saving ruler of God's kingdom. In the Old Testament, we see the foundations of this message and we learn who God is, what he does and how he works. God has a relationship with his people based on his promises. In the New Testament, we see the fulfilment of these promises in Jesus Christ. By his life, death and resurrection, Jesus began God's kingdom, and he will return to establish it forever.

Reading the Bible using COMA

The best way to get to know the Bible is to read it often and pray that God will make its meaning clear to you. A helpful process to use when you are reading a Bible passage is the COMA method. It takes into account the message of the Bible that has been outlined during *The Bible Overview* presentations. Using an approach such as this will help us to understand each section of the Bible properly as part of the whole book, and avoid common errors that are made in Bible reading.

There are four stages to the COMA approach, which are simply four things to consider as you read a passage of the Bible:

Context
The context of a passage is the answer to the question: "Where does it fit?" To answer this, you need to address the following issues:
- Where does the content of this passage fit into the bigger story of the Bible?
- What has happened so far?
- What is still to come?
- What is the main thrust of this book of the Bible?

Observation
Observation refers to *how* something is communicated. It's worth asking questions such as:
- What type of writing is this book/passage?

- Is there any way that the passage can be naturally broken down into smaller sections?
- Are there any words that seem particularly important, or that are hard to understand?
- How is this writing structured? Is it a poem? A proverb? A letter?

Meaning

That brings us to meaning ("What does this passage mean?"). Here, we draw together the things we have already found out, and ask the questions:

- What does this passage tell us about God, Jesus, God's people, or the world?
- What might this passage have meant to its original hearers?
- How can we sum up the meaning of this passage in our own words?

Application

The final stage of the process is application ("Why does this matter?"). Ask yourself:

- How does the message of this passage instruct us today?
- Does it require us to change our understanding of who God is, what God does or how God works in relation to his people or the world?
- Does it require that we change the attitudes we hold, or the way we live?

matthiasmedia

Matthias Media is an evangelical publishing ministry that seeks to persuade all Christians of the truth of God's purposes in Jesus Christ as revealed in the Bible, and equip them with high-quality resources, so that by the work of the Holy Spirit they will:

- abandon their lives to the honour and service of Christ in daily holiness and decision-making
- pray constantly in Christ's name for the fruitfulness and growth of his gospel
- speak the Bible's life-changing word whenever and however they can—in the home, in the world and in the fellowship of his people.

It was in 1988 that we first started pursuing this mission, and in God's kindness we now have more than 300 different ministry resources being used all over the world. These resources range from Bible studies and books through to training courses and audio sermons.

To find out more about our large range of very useful resources, and to access samples and free downloads, visit our website:

www.matthiasmedia.com.au

How to buy our resources

1. Direct from us over the internet:
   – in the US: www.matthiasmedia.com
   – in Australia and the rest of the world: www.matthiasmedia.com.au

2. Direct from us by phone:
   – in the US: 1 866 407 4530
   – in Australia: 1800 814 360 (Sydney: 9663 1478)
   – international: +61-2-9663-1478

3. Through a range of outlets in various parts of the world. **Visit www.matthiasmedia.com.au/international.php** for details about recommended retailers in your part of the world, including www.thegoodbook.co.uk in the United Kingdom.

4. Trade enquiries can be addressed to:
   – in the US and Canada: sales@matthiasmedia.com
   – in Australia and the rest of the world: sales@matthiasmedia.com.au

Register at our website for our **free** regular email update to receive information about the latest new resources, **exclusive special offers**, and free articles to help you grow in your Christian life and ministry.

Six Steps to Reading Your Bible

Whatever your current Bible reading habits (or lack of them), and whatever your level of knowledge and confidence, *Six Steps to Reading Your Bible* will help you make progress in getting into your Bible. The course is especially designed for use in small groups, and utilizes a mix of video instruction, fun skits, Bible study, discussion, practical exercises, prayer and home assignments that will help you on the road to establishing a new and more enjoyable Bible reading habit.

Six Steps to Reading your Bible is a six-session course, best undertaken in a small group (of 6-10 people). To run the course you will need:

- a workbook for each person, which also contains notes for group leaders
- a DVD to use in the group.

Full of Promise

Do you want to:

- Understand the overall story of the Old Testament?
- See how the Old Testament connects with the new?
- Read the Old Testament in just 8 sittings?

Here's the study that does it!

In just eight studies, you'll go on a whirlwind tour of the entire Old Testament, seeing how the whole magnificent story holds together, and how it repeatedly foreshadows and points forward to Jesus. We've received many notes and calls from people saying that *Full of Promise* has opened their eyes to the Old Testament for the first time, and given them confidence to go back and read it for themselves.

FOR MORE INFORMATION OR TO ORDER CONTACT:

Matthias Media
Telephone: +61-2-9663-1478
Facsimile: +61-2-9663-3265
Email: sales@matthiasmedia.com.au
www.matthiasmedia.com.au

Matthias Media (USA)
Telephone: 1-866-407-4530
Facsimile: 724-964-8166
Email: sales@matthiasmedia.com
www.matthiasmedia.com